HOME

STENCILLING

HOME
STENCILLING

Contents

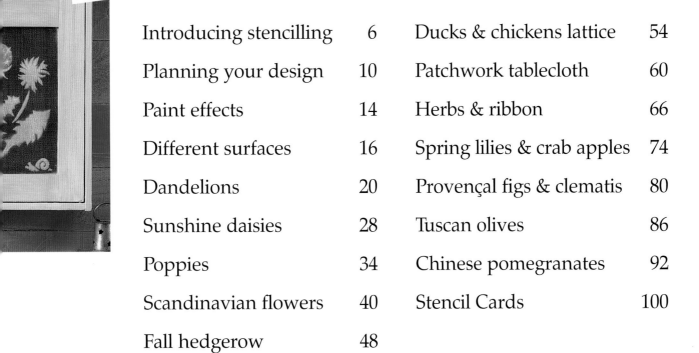

Introducing stencilling

Once you begin stencilling you will be amazed at the wonderful results you can obtain quite easily and without spending a great deal of money. This book introduces six themed projects and provides ready-to-use stencils that can be used with numerous variations in design — just follow the step-by-step features and simple instructions. With very little paint and only a few pieces of equipment you can achieve stunning results. Have fun!

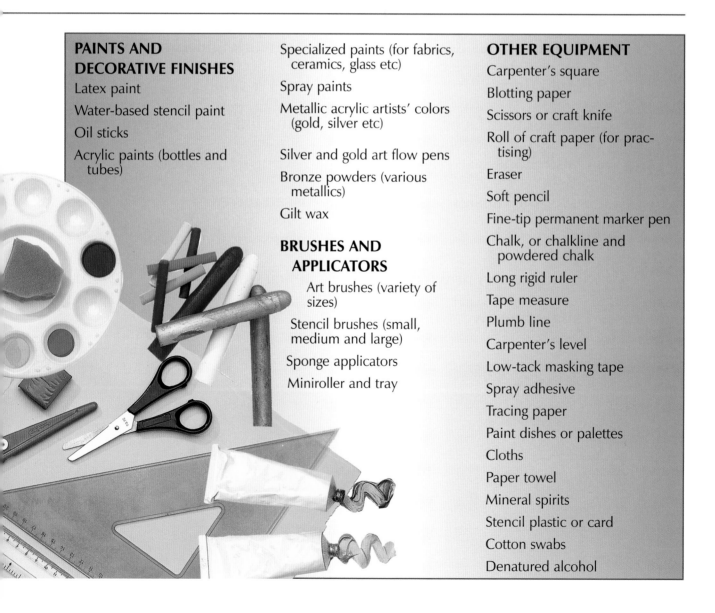

PAINTS AND DECORATIVE FINISHES

Latex paint

Water-based stencil paint

Oil sticks

Acrylic paints (bottles and tubes)

Specialized paints (for fabrics, ceramics, glass etc)

Spray paints

Metallic acrylic artists' colors (gold, silver etc)

Silver and gold art flow pens

Bronze powders (various metallics)

Gilt wax

BRUSHES AND APPLICATORS

Art brushes (variety of sizes)

Stencil brushes (small, medium and large)

Sponge applicators

Miniroller and tray

OTHER EQUIPMENT

Carpenter's square

Blotting paper

Scissors or craft knife

Roll of craft paper (for practising)

Eraser

Soft pencil

Fine-tip permanent marker pen

Chalk, or chalkline and powdered chalk

Long rigid ruler

Tape measure

Plumb line

Carpenter's level

Low-tack masking tape

Spray adhesive

Tracing paper

Paint dishes or palettes

Cloths

Paper towel

Mineral spirits

Stencil plastic or card

Cotton swabs

Denatured alcohol

CUTTING OUT STENCILS

The stencils at the back of the book are all designed to use separately or together to create many different pattern combinations. Cut along the dotted lines of the individual stencils and make sure you transfer the reference code onto each one with a permanent pen. Carefully remove the cutout pieces of the stencil. Apply 2″ (50 mm) strips of tracing paper around the edges using masking tape; this will help to prevent smudging paint onto your surface.

DUPLICATING STENCILS

Stencil plastic (Mylar) can be used; or card stock wiped over with linseed oil, which will harden when left to dry and make the surface waterproof. Place the cutout stencil on top. Carefully trace around the cutout shapes with a permanent pen. Cut along the lines with a craft knife and remove the pieces. You may prefer to trace the stencil design first, then transfer your tracing stencil plastic or onto card stock.

REPAIRING STENCILS

Stencils may become damaged and torn from mishandling, or if the cutouts have not been removed carefully, but they are easy to repair. Keeping the stencil perfectly flat, cover both sides of the tear with masking tape. Then carefully remove any excess tape with a craft knife.

LOOKING AFTER STENCILS

Stencils have a long life if cared for correctly. Before cleaning make sure you remove any tape or tracing paper that has been added. Remove any excess paint before it dries, and wipe the stencil with a damp cloth after each use. If water-based or acrylic paint has dried and hardened, soften it with water and ease it off gently with a craft knife. Then use a small amount of denatured alcohol on a cloth to remove the rest. An oil-based paint can be removed by simply wiping over the stencil with mineral spirits on a cloth. Stencils should be dried thoroughly before storing flat between sheets of waxed paper.

Getting started

MAKING A SPONGE APPLICATOR

Sponging your stencil is one of the easiest methods, but you may prefer to use a stencil brush, especially for fine detail. Using a piece of upholstery foam or very dense bath sponge, cut pieces ½–2 " (12–50 mm) wide and approximately 2" (50 mm) long. Hold the four corners together and secure with tape to form a pad. You can also round off the ends with scissors or a craft knife and trim to a smooth finish. The small-ended applicators can be used for tiny, intricate patterns.

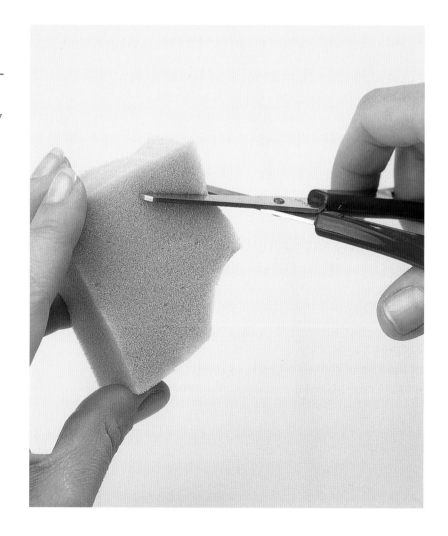

HOW TO USE WATER-BASED PAINT

Water-based paints are easy and economical to use and have the advantage of drying quickly. For professional-looking stencils, do not load your sponge or brush too heavily or you will not achieve a soft, shaded finish. Paint that is too watery will seep under the stencil edges and smudge. If the paint is too heavy you will obtain a heavy block effect rather than the soft stippling you require.

HOW TO USE OIL STICKS

Oil sticks may seem expensive, but in fact go a long way. They take longer to dry, allowing you to blend colors very effectively. Oil sticks are applied with a stencil brush and you need to have a different brush for each color. Break the seal as instructed on the stick and rub a patch of the color onto a palette, allowing space to blend colors. As the stencil sticks dry slowly, you need to lift the stencil off cleanly, and replace to continue the pattern.

PRACTISING PAINTING STENCILS

Roll out some craft paper onto a table and select the stencil you wish to practise with. Using spray adhesive, lightly spray the back of your stencil and place it into position on the paper. Prepare your paint on a palette. Dab your sponge or brush into the paint and offload excess paint onto scrap paper. Apply color over the stencil in a light coat to create an even stippled effect. You can always stencil on a little more paint if a stronger effect is needed, but if you over apply it in the first place it is very difficult to remove. Keep separate sponges for different colors.

Planning your design

Before starting to stencil take time to plan your design. Decide where you want to use the patterns, then work out how to position the stencils so that the design will fit around obstacles such as doorways and corners. The techniques shown here will help you to undertake the job with a systematic approach.

PUTTING PATTERN PIECES TOGETHER

1 Before you apply your design, stencil a sample onto craft paper. Mark the centre and baseline of the design on the paper and put together your pattern pieces. You can then work out the size of the design, how it will fit into the space available and the distance required between repeats.

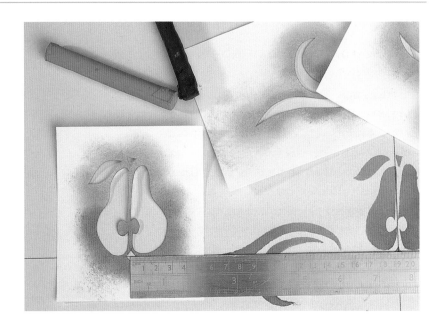

2 You can avoid stencilling around a corner by working out the number of pattern repeats needed, and allowing extra space either between repeats or within the pattern. Creating vertical lines through the pattern will allow you to stretch it evenly.

MARKING BASELINES AND HORIZONTAL LINES

Select your stencil area, and take a measure from the ceiling, doorframe, window or edging, bearing in mind the depth of your stencil. Using a carpenter's level, mark out a horizontal line. You can then extend this by using a chalkline or long ruler with chalk or a soft pencil.

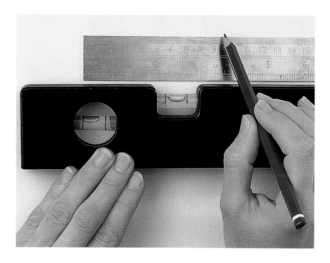

MARKING VERTICAL LINES

If you need to work out the vertical position for a stencil, hang a plumb line above the stencilling area and use a ruler to draw a vertical line with chalk or a soft pencil. You will need to use this method when creating an all-over wallpaper design.

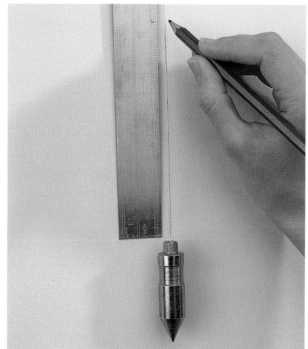

FIXING THE STENCIL INTO PLACE

Lightly spray the back of the stencil with spray adhesive, then put it in position and smooth it down carefully. You can use low-tack masking tape if you prefer, but take care not to damage the surface to be stencilled; keep the whole stencil flat to prevent paint seeping underneath.

MARKING THE STENCIL FOR
A PATTERN REPEAT

Attach a border of tracing paper to each edge
of the stencil. Position the next pattern and
overlap the tracing paper onto the previous
design, tracing over the edge of it. By matching
the tracing with the previous pattern as you
work along you will be able to align and repeat
the stencil at the same intervals.

COPING WITH CORNERS

Stencil around corners after you have finished
the rest of the design, having measured to leave
the correct space for the corner pattern before you
do so. Then bend the stencil into the corner and
mask off one side of it. Stencil the open side and
allow the paint to dry, then mask off this half and
stencil the other part to complete the design.

MASKING OFF PART OF A STENCIL

Use low-tack masking tape to mask out small
or intricate areas of stencil. You can also use
ordinary masking tape, but remove excess
stickiness first by peeling it on and off your skin
or a cloth once or twice. To block off inside shapes
and large areas, cut out pieces of tracing paper to
the appropriate size and fix them on top with
spray adhesive.

MITERING STENCIL PATTERNS

1 When you are stencilling a continuous pattern and need to make a corner, mask off the stencil by marking a 45-degree angle at both ends of the stencil with a permanent pen. Mask along this line with a piece of masking tape or tracing paper.

2 Make sure the baselines of the stencil on both sides of the corner are the same distance from the edge, and that they cross at the corner. Put the diagonal end of the stencil right into the corner and apply the paint. Turn the stencil sideways to align the other diagonal end of the stencil and turn the corner.

Paint effects

CHOOSING COLORS

Take care to choose appropriate colors to create the effect you want. Stencil a practice piece onto paper and try a variation of colors to ensure you are pleased with the result. Different colors can make a design look entirely different. Use spray adhesive to fix your practice paper onto the surface on which you wish to produce the design so that you can assess its effect before applying the stencil.

APPLYING WATER-BASED COLORS

Water-based paint dries quickly, so it tends to layer rather than blend. It is best applied by using a swirling movement or gently dabbing, depending on the finished effect you wish to create. Once you have applied a light base color, you can add a darker edge for shading. Alternatively, leave some of the stencil bare and add a different tone to that area to obtain a shaded or highlighted appearance.

BLENDING OIL-STICK COLORS

Oil sticks mix together smoothly and are perfect for blending colors. Place the colors separately on your palette and mix them with white to obtain a variety of tones or blend them together to create new colors. You can also blend by applying one coat into another with a stippling motion while stencilling. Blending looks most effective when applying a pale base coat, then shading on top with a darker color.

HIGHLIGHTING

A simple way to add highlighting to your design is first to paint in your stencil in a light tone of your main color, then carefully lift the stencil and move it down a fraction. Then stencil in a darker shade; this leaves the highlighted areas around the top edges of the pattern.

GILDING

After painting your stencil use gold to highlight the edges. Load a fine art brush with gold acrylic paint and carefully outline the top edges of the pattern. Use one quick brush stroke for each pattern repeat, keeping in the same direction. Other methods are to blow bronze powder onto the wet paint, draw around the pattern with a gold flow pen, or smudge on gilt wax cream, then buff to a high sheen.

APPLYING SPRAY PAINTS

Spray paints are ideal on glass, wood, metal, plastic and ceramic surfaces. They are quick to apply and fast drying, but cannot be blended, although you can achieve subtle shaded effects. Apply the paint in several thin coats. Mask off a large area around the design to protect it from the spray, which tends to drift. Try to use sprays out of doors or in a well-ventilated area. Some spray paints are non-toxic, making them ideal for children's furniture.

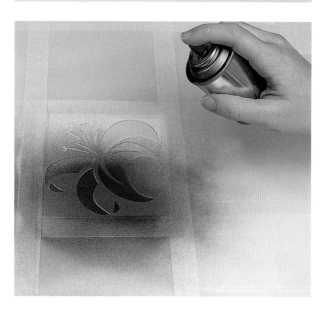

Different surfaces

RAW WOOD

Rub the wood surface down to a smooth finish. Then fix the stencil in place and paint with a thin base coat of white, so that the stencil colors will stand out well when applied. Leave the stencil in place and allow to dry thoroughly, then apply your stencil colors in the normal way. When completely dry you can apply a coat of light wax or varnish to protect your stencil.

PAINTED WOOD

If you are painting wood or manufactured wood products (MDF) prior to stencilling, seal it with a coat of acrylic primer before adding a base coat of latex or acrylic paint. If the base coat is dark, stencil a thin coat of white paint on top. Apply your stencil and, if required, protect with a coat of clear varnish when it is completely dry.

FABRIC

Use special fabric paint for stencilling on fabric and follow the manufacturer's instructions carefully. Place card or blotting paper behind the fabric while working and keep the material taut. If you are painting a dark fabric, best results are achieved by stencilling first with white or a lighter shade. Heat seal the design following the manufacturer's instructions.

CERAMICS

Use special ceramic paints to work directly onto glazed ceramic tiles, and unglazed ceramics such as terra cotta. Make sure all surfaces are clean, so that the stencils can be fixed easily. Apply the paint with a brush, sponge, spray or miniroller. Ceramic paints are durable and washable, and full manufacturer's instructions are given on the container.

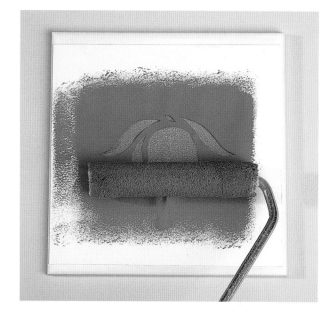

GLASS

Before applying the stencil make sure the glass is clean, spray on a light coat of adhesive and place the stencil in position. Spray on water-based or ceramic paint, remove the stencil and allow to dry. If you wish to stencil drinking glasses, use special non-toxic and water-resistant glass paints. An etched-glass look with stencils on windows, doors and mirrors can be achieved with a variety of materials.

PAINTED SURFACES

Stencils can be applied to surfaces painted with flat or satin latex emulsion, oil-based scumble glazes, acrylic glazes and varnishes, and to matt wallpaper. If you wish to decorate a gloss surface, stencil first with an acrylic primer, leave to dry and then stencil the colors on top. Surfaces to be stencilled need to be smooth so that the stencil can lie flat.

FLOWER
POWER

Flowers have always been a source of inspiration for artists and interior designers. Their varied forms and colors provide an endless palette of ideas for stencilling. This chapter shows a range of different flower stencils, from the humble dandelion to the exotic poppy. Each project shows how both the flower itself and its foliage work together, making a wonderful pattern to suit different rooms and styles in your home.

Dandelions

Most gardeners have a love/hate relationship with the dandelion — this flower grows and spreads like wildfire, plaguing lawns with long roots that are extremely difficult to dig up. To children, however, dandelions are heaven-sent to "tell the time" by blowing the feathery seed heads on summer afternoons. A mesh cupboard is an ideal piece for this project, giving it a "potting shed" feel. The leaves and flowers are joined to create dandelion plants growing from the bottom of the cupboard, with seeds floating above and a snail sneaking in.

PAINT COLOR GUIDE
White spray paint

DECORATING THE CUPBOARD DOORS

1 Paint the cupboard's wood sections with an all-in-one primer/undercoat in white. Paint a couple of layers of white latex on top. You may be able to get away with just one layer depending how thick the paint is.

2 Make up a wash by diluting a stone-colored latex with water. Put the color on and carefully drag it off with a dry brush to give an "old" wood effect. Work the paint in the direction of the wood sections of the cupboard, emphasizing the joints. When dry, give the wood a few coats of varnish.

3 The door knobs are stones with holes through the middle, tied on with string.

4 Paint the dandelion stencils on the mesh using white spray paint. Practise on a spare piece of mesh. If you make a mistake, mix some silver and black paint to neaten the edges.

The dandelion plants are built up by combining the different leaves and stalks (used in reverse and upside down), topped with flowers and seed heads (dandelion clocks). The seeds are in the same pattern on each side although the overall look is random.

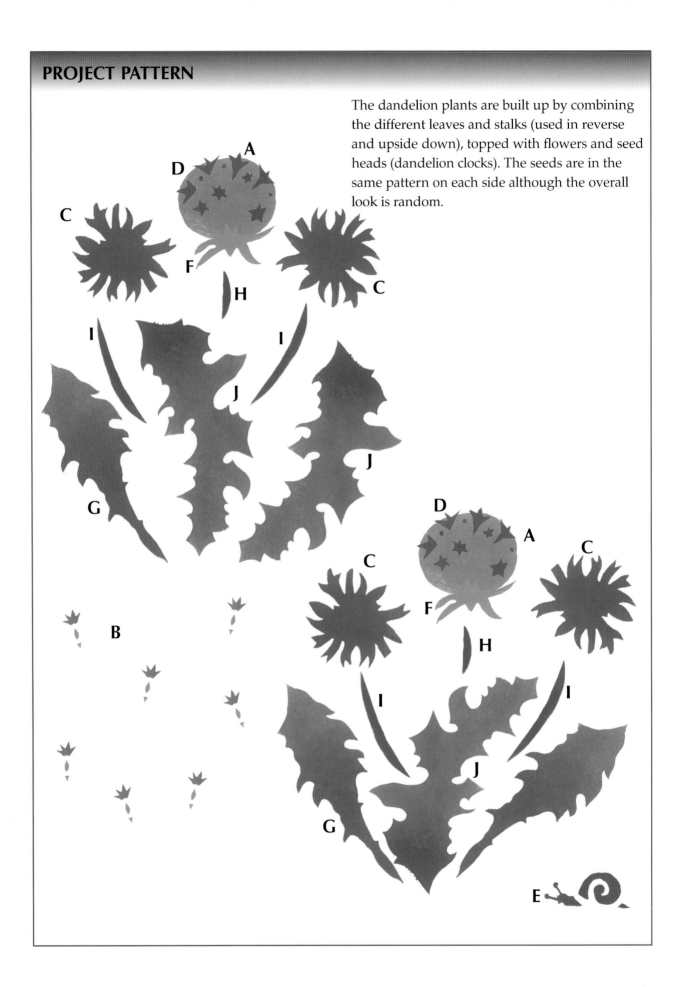

SPRAYING THE BASE COLOR

Make sure that the stencils are fixed securely with spray adhesive, then spray the paint in thin layers to give a well-defined edge. Spray the background of the seed head (stencil D) lightly to give the faint impression of a globe before painting the individual seeds stencil A on top.

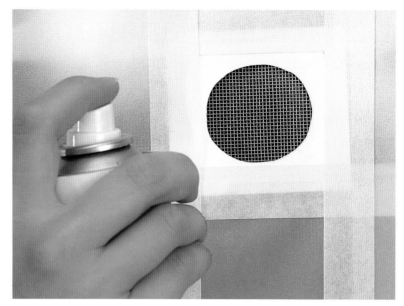

BUILDING UP LAYERS

To achieve a more opaque finish, spray lightly building up thin layers. Make sure that each element is dry before you move on to the next. Be careful not to over spray as the mesh holes can clog up easily.

CREATING THE SNAIL STENCIL

Use the snail (stencil E) to create a trail round a pot, along the front of shelves or on top of skirting boards. A simple element in a single color can be low key or dramatic depending on the color you use and how densely you apply it.

Dandelions variations

This project provides endless opportunities for creative decoration.
You can use greens and yellows to form realistic-looking dandelion
plants or, as shown here using greens, turquoises and blues,
choose the individual elements to build up many other designs.
Do not be afraid to experiment with the different shapes as pure
pattern rather than restricting yourself to the realistic growth
pattern of the actual plant.

Snail trail (stencil E)

Leaf border (stencil J)

Star edging (stencil A)

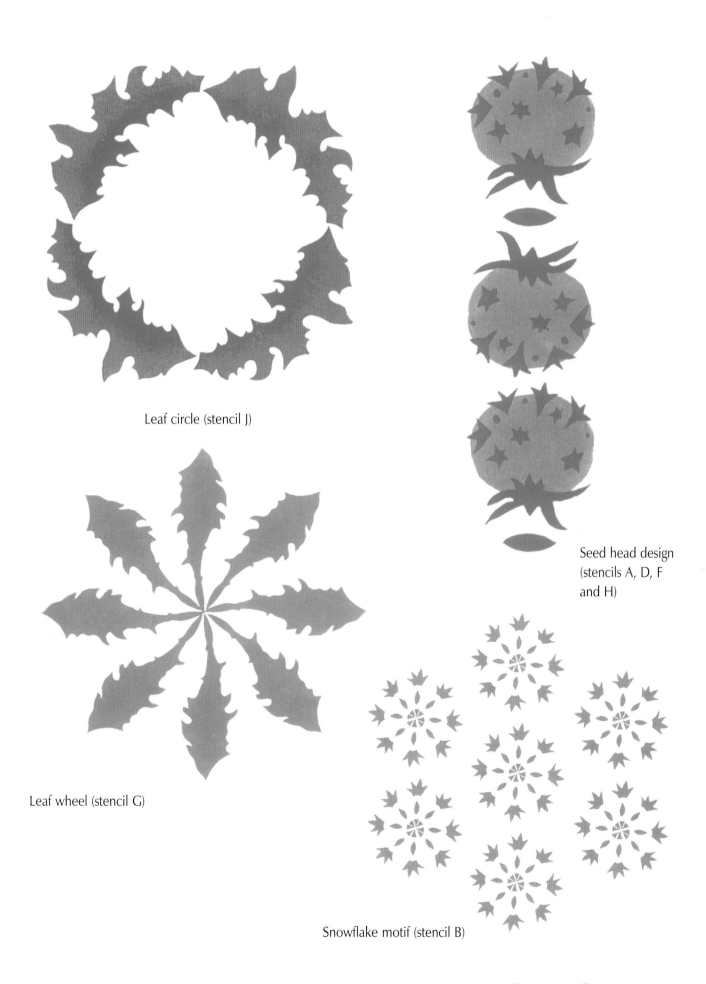

Leaf circle (stencil J)

Seed head design
(stencils A, D, F
and H)

Leaf wheel (stencil G)

Snowflake motif (stencil B)

Seed head design (stencils A, D, F and H)

Flower and stalk repeat (stencils C and I)

Flower corner (stencil C)

Star medallion (stencil A)

Narrow leaf diamond border (stencil G)

Regimental seeds row (stencil B)

Leaf border (stencil J)

Seed square repeat (stencil B)

Sunshine daisies

This sunny daisy design seems to represent all the warmth of summer. Stencilled onto table linen these flowers will brighten any meal and bring glowing compliments from guests. Placemats could be stencilled to match the tablecloth. Stencilling onto fabric requires confidence as mistakes cannot be wiped away, but with a little practice this project is well within the reach of a beginner.

The table linen here has been painted in warm yellows, but the flowers would look equally striking in other bright colors.

PAINT COLOR GUIDE
White
Yellow
Red
Green

STENCILLING ONTO FABRIC

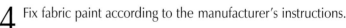

1 Wash the fabric before painting to remove any finishes. Press well.

2 When stencilling on fabric be particularly careful to use as dry a brush as possible to avoid paint seeping under the stencil. Fabric paints are available in a more limited range of colors, so mix the yellow and red paints for further warm yellows and oranges.

3 Position stem stencils B and D first before placing the flowers and leaves.

4 Fix fabric paint according to the manufacturer's instructions.

POSITIONING THE STENCIL

Use parts of the stem (stencil B) and flower stencils to make a bunch, masking areas not to be painted. Hold the stencil in place on the fabric with spray adhesive. Reposition the stencils carefully for each subsequent color you apply.

PAINTING THE STENCIL

When working on a colored fabric, paint the whole design in white before applying the colors. Allow the white paint to dry and fix according to the manufacturer's instructions before adding the colors. This gives a good background for the subsequent colors.

ADDING THE COLORS

Use a clean sponge to apply pale yellow for the petals. Let the yellow paint dry and fix it before adding more colors. Paint a rich orange-red in the centre for the stamens. Overlap the colors to effect a gradual change.

Daisies variations

The Sunshine Daisies stencils look good on walls and furniture as well as on fabric. Paint a border of flower heads in the breakfast room to complement your tablecloth. The circle of leaves is formed by overlapping a leaf stencil, taking care not to paint over the previous leaf. Try painting the flowers in different colors and flipping the stencils to create a posy.

Leaf circle (stencil C)

Daisies (stencils A, B and E)

Bunch of daisies (stencils A and E)

Daisy edging (stencil D)

Leaf border (stencil C)

Daisy and leaf border (stencils A and B)

Climbing leaves frame (stencil B)

Two daisies border
(stencils A, B and E)

Daisy border (stencil E)

Daisy chain
(stencils B and E)

Poppies

Poppies conjure up the quintessential hazy feeling of a high summer's day. In this project the combination of yellow ochre, deep purple, red and fiery orange creates a harmonious warm atmosphere. Spiky leaves, curvaceous poppy flowers with dark seductive centres, rounded seed heads, gently bending buds and bumble bees fuse to form a sympathetic union of shapes. Together the colors and shapes convey the feeling of walking through a golden field of corn, dotted with the richness of red and orange wildflowers.

PAINT COLOR GUIDE

Deep purple

Dark red

Fiery orange

PAINTING THE FRAME

1 Paint the frame with all-in-one primer/undercoat and then paint two layers of yellow ochre latex paint.

2 Mix up a wash, with the consistency of light cream, using a burnt umber acrylic and latex glaze. Gently apply the wash with big brushstrokes, working across the frame so that there is a hint of color.

3 Apply the large poppy (stencils E, G and F) in the corners of the frame and add the other elements in a random pattern. Finish the frame by painting the inner and outer edges with a rich red to give the sides definition.

In this random design the most difficult element is the poppy flower. Place stencil E first and then put stencil G carefully on top. Finish with stencil F, to complete the flower.

POSITIONING
WITH CUTOUTS

To position the stencils make cutouts
in paper and move the shapes
around until you are happy with the
design. Start with the larger shapes
to get the pattern going and fill in
the gaps with the smaller ones. Let
some shapes overlap the frame.

CHECKING WITH
TRACING PAPER

To create the large poppy petals
apply stencil G over stencil E.
Position the two parts by using
tracing paper to make a drawing of
the way that the shapes fit together.
After stencilling the bottom shape
(stencil E), slide the top shape
(stencil G) under the tracing paper,
then remove the paper.

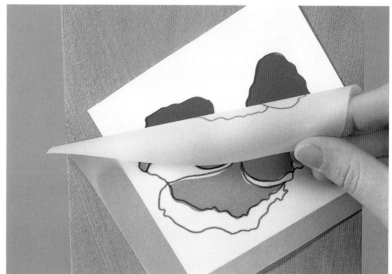

KEEPING COLORS CLEAN

When using two colors within the
same shape work from opposite
ends of the stencil with them.
Combine the colors in the middle
with a different brush to keep the
tones clean and clear.

Poppies variations

By adding pinks and yellow ochre to your palette of rich reds, oranges and purples you can move the design of this project towards the Orient to give a more mysterious feel or to India for a more exotic look. If you are adventurous you could make realistic poppy plants look as if they are growing out of the skirting boards or create entire poppy fields on the walls.

Seed head edging (stencil C)

Poppy centre
design
(stencil F)

Leaf zigzag (stencil A)

Bee repeat (stencil B)

Poppy bud and leaf tile border (stencils A and D)

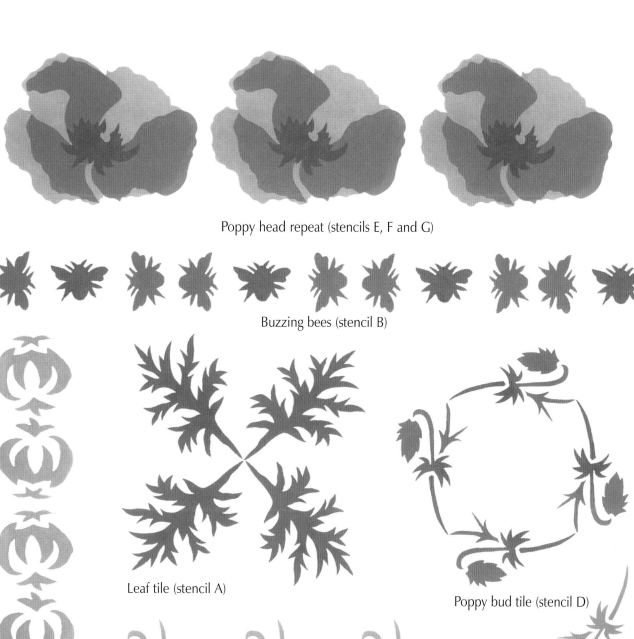

Poppy head repeat (stencils E, F and G)

Buzzing bees (stencil B)

Leaf tile (stencil A)

Poppy bud tile (stencil D)

Linked poppy bud border (stencil D)

Seed head stripe
(stencil C)

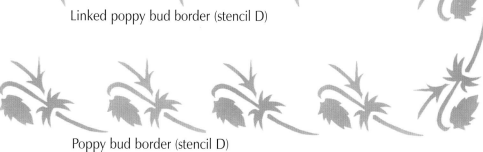

Poppy bud border (stencil D)

Scandinavian flowers

These Scandinavian-style stencils were inspired by the architectural detail on a 19th-century Swedish house decorated in the Gustavian style. Their charm lies in their simplicity and the wonderful muted colors of the traditional Scandinavian palette. Soft grey-greens and blues combine to make this a very restful room. The border has been created by combining the leaf stencils and the wall is covered with individual tumbling leaves. To create a completely different look try painting these stencils in strong bright colors.

PAINT COLOR GUIDE

Cream

Deep blue-green

Mid blue-green

Pale blue-green

Blue-grey

PLANNING A BORDER

1 Carefully position the individual pieces to make a stylized border. The design here uses the three leaf stencils (C, D and E) and part of the hanging bells (stencil F).

2 Draw the design on a sheet of paper before you begin and note how the pieces are arranged. This will make it much easier when you come to put them on the wall.

3 Measure the distance to be covered carefully so that the pattern will fit, working each part of the design from its centre.

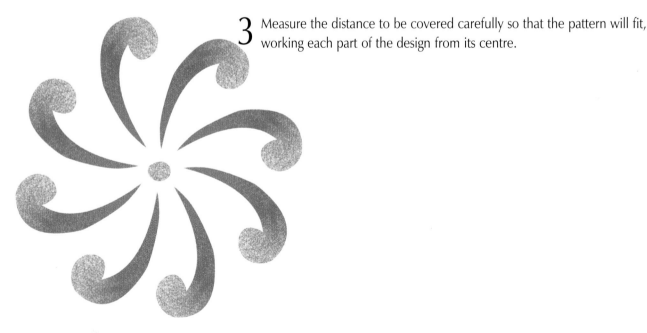

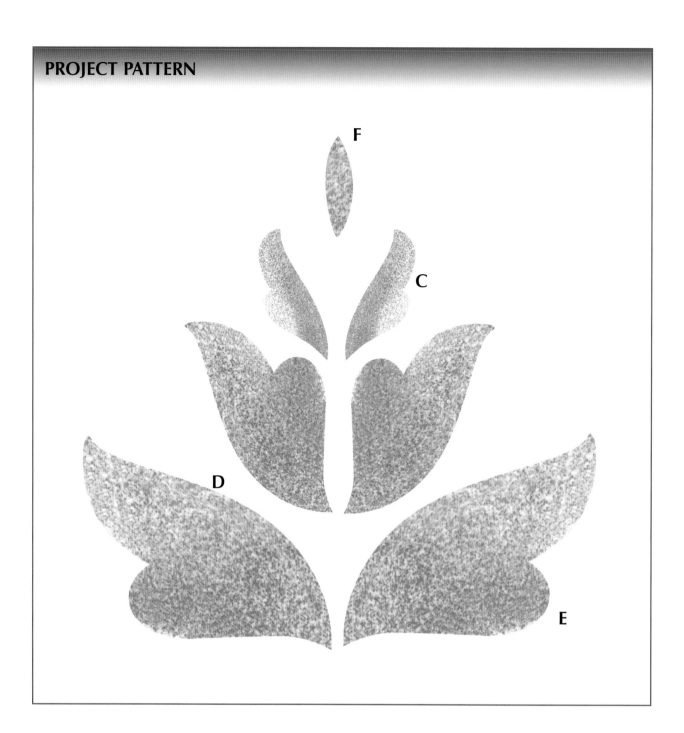

POSITIONING THE STENCIL

Mark the centre of the wall for the position of the first stencil. Measure the wall so that the design fits and you are not left without enough room to place a complete design. This will save you bending the stencils around a corner.

ALIGNING THE STENCILS

The complete design is formed by painting leaf (stencil E), flipping it over and painting it again as a mirror image, and repeating the process with leaves (D and C). This is topped with the drop shape from stencil F. Measure from a central vertical line.

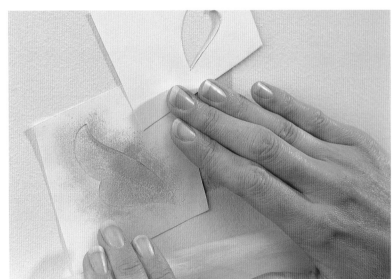

PAINTING

Use a sponge for each color. Begin with the lowest leaf, painting in the order blue-grey, dark blue-green, mid blue-green and pale blue-green, blending from leaf to leaf. This gives weight and interest to the design.

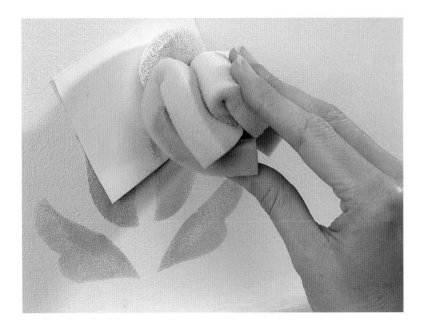

Scandinavian flowers variations

Try playing with these stencils to make interesting patterns. You can use just one leaf stencil to create a number of different borders. Flip the stencil over, turn it round or overlap the images. Use the hearts and leaves to give a "country" feel or the "comma", ribbon and hanging bells for a more formal effect. Subtle color combinations can make simple designs look elegant and sophisticated.

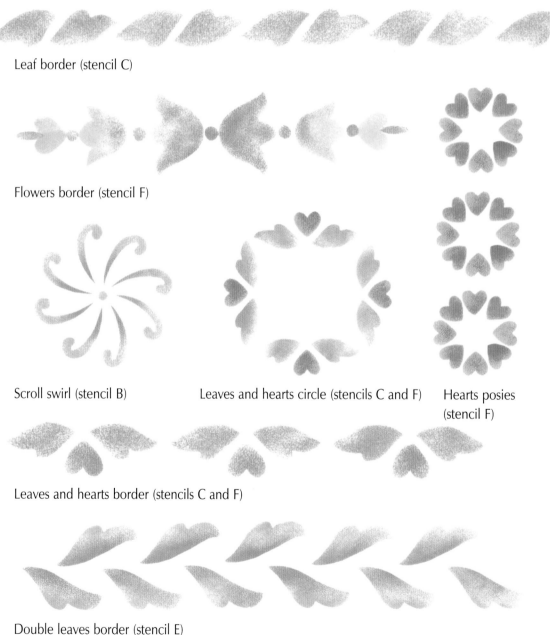

Double rope border (stencil A)

Leaf border (stencil C)

Flowers border (stencil F)

Scroll swirl (stencil B)

Leaves and hearts circle (stencils C and F)

Hearts posies (stencil F)

Leaves and hearts border (stencils C and F)

Double leaves border (stencil E)

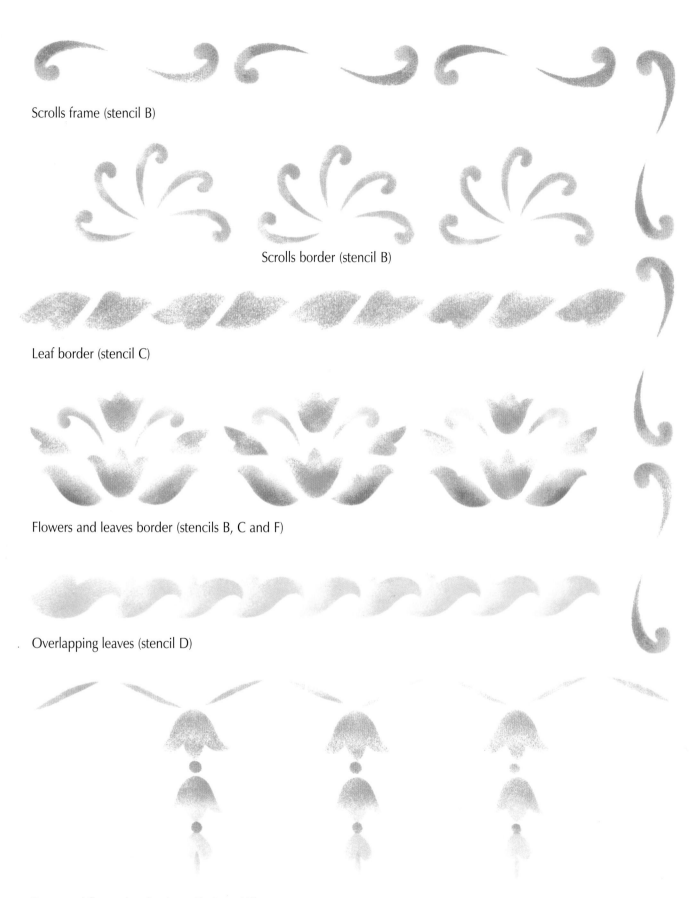

Scrolls frame (stencil B)

Scrolls border (stencil B)

Leaf border (stencil C)

Flowers and leaves border (stencils B, C and F)

Overlapping leaves (stencil D)

Rope and flower border (stencils A and F)

RUSTIC
CHARM

Country life is the theme of this selection of stencils. These designs celebrate that wholesome world where nature is honoured and where simple charm is preferred to sophisticated style. The honest appeal of these patterns gives them a calming air that makes them perfect for creating a sense of tranquility. From chickens and ducks to fall berries and traditional herbs, the designs in this chapter will bring a breath of country air into your home — wherever you may live.

Fall hedgerow

Capture the richness of fall with these hedgerow stencils of rich juicy blackberries, ripe rose hips and leaves changing color from green to russet. This archway decorated with fruit and leaves trailing haphazardly around its frame perfectly evokes the season of "mists and mellow fruitfulness". The stencils are ideal for making matching, but not identical, designs in other areas of the room. Use random combinations of patterns to paint a border or highlight another feature, such as a window.

PAINT COLOR GUIDE

Yellow ochre

Plum

Bright red

Fresh green

Warm yellow

ARRANGING THE STENCILS

1 Arranging these stencils requires a little practice. Start by painting one stencil, perhaps some leaves. Then hold another of the designs to it to decide which section to paint next; choose all or part of a design, whichever looks right in that position.

2 Continue building up your design in this way. The patterns can be made to curve around an arch, make a border or trail round a corner.

POSITIONING THE STENCILS

Position these stencils individually to curve around the archway. A random arrangement will look more natural than a repetition of the same designs. Start with one of the stencils, adding all or parts of the other designs to form a pleasing arrangement.

PAINTING THE STENCIL

Paint the blackberries (stencil B) with the plum paint and the rose hips (stencil E) with bright red. Use yellow and green for the flowers and leaves. Blend and shade colors to enhance the effect. A touch of red on the edge of a leaf works well.

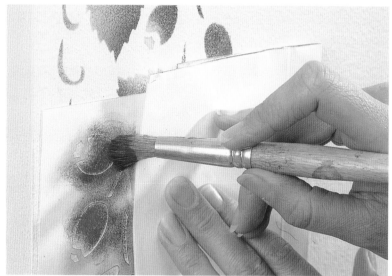

EXTRA DETAILS

Use parts of the stencil to add extra details and balance the design. A single flower or fruit may be all that is needed. Mask off areas of the stencil that you are not using.

Fall hedgerow variations

The look of the hedgerow stencils can be changed by masking some details and combining the leaves from one stencil with the flowers from another. Or choose a single simple motif and repeat it, as shown in the blackberry border. The "triangular" rose hip cluster has one rosehip omitted so that it fits neatly together. Vary the intensity of the colors you use, experiment with the various stencils and colors, and find your own style.

Flower circlet (stencil C)

Flower border (stencil C)

Rose hip drop
(stencil E)

Flower border (stencils A and D)

Blackberries and leaves (stencils B, D and E)

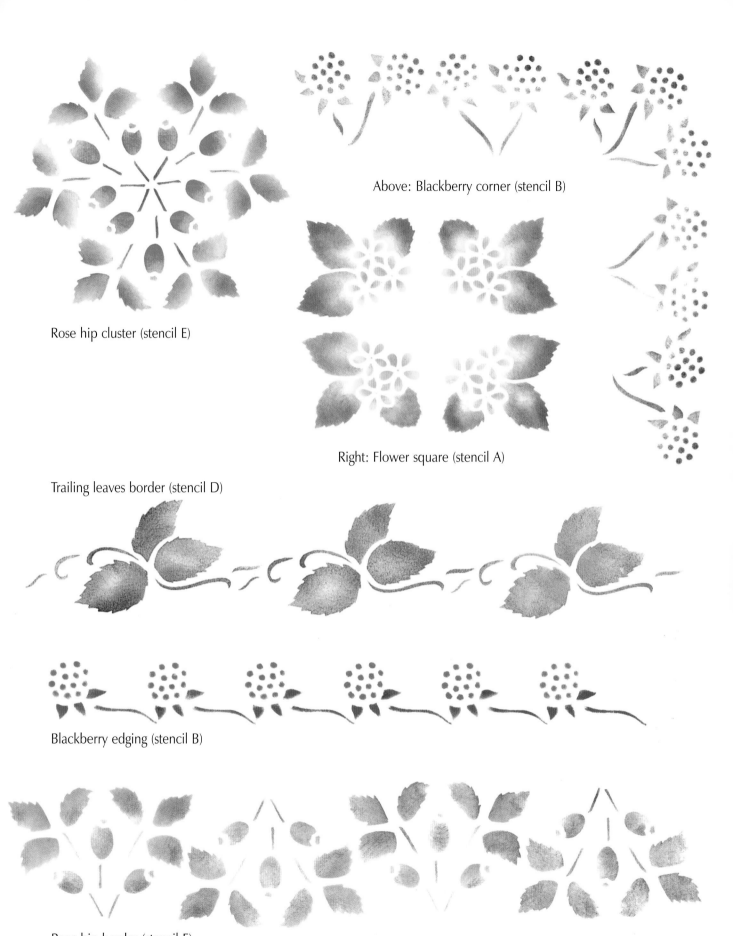

Rose hip cluster (stencil E)

Above: Blackberry corner (stencil B)

Right: Flower square (stencil A)

Trailing leaves border (stencil D)

Blackberry edging (stencil B)

Rose hip border (stencil E)

Ducks & chickens lattice

Warm, rich purple, terra cotta and earth tones conjure up a cosy farmhouse feel, with ducks and chickens in brilliant gold for a touch of sophistication. These traditional rustic colors immediately suggest a welcoming atmosphere. Just imagine the smells of freshly baked bread wafting through the kitchen and smoking log fires — utter bliss. You can use this project to create a tiled effect, transforming a town kitchen or breakfast room, or enhancing your rural surroundings, quickly and easily.

PAINT COLOR GUIDE

Muted purple

Dusky cream

Terracotta

Gold

PAINTING A TILED EFFECT

1 Paint the wall in a dark cream latex to simulate a grout color.

2 Work out the size of your tiles. Draw them out on the wall, with the aid of a carpenter's level, leaving a ⅜" (1 cm) gap in between each tile.

3 Divide a roll of masking tape lengthwise using a craft knife so that you have tape ⅜" (1 cm) wide. Stick the tape where you require the grout lines.

4 Mix up different shades of latex paint with matt glaze and paint the tiles. Remove the tape. You will be left with squares of color.

5 Stencil the lattice first (stencils E and F) and fill in the round blank space with feathers, ducks or chickens.

6 Give the whole surface a couple of layers of varnish.

The lattice tiles in the photograph on the previous page are put together as shown here ready for your choice of motif in the centre.

F   E   F

E   E

F   E   F

POSITIONING THE LATTICE

To position the lattice (stencils E and F) mark the stencil card with permanent marker to correspond with the tile lines behind. It does not matter if the stencils are not exactly straight, it will just add to the hand-painted look, but it is worth trying to keep them more or less in line.

APPLYING METALLIC GOLD PAINT

Using a metallic paint is slightly more difficult than an ordinary paint. You need to apply it more thickly to achieve an opaque look that really shines. Work on two tiles at the same time so that each stage can dry and you do not smudge the work you have just done.

PAINTING THE BIRDS

To emphasize the gold and to give the chickens and ducks depth it is a good idea to stencil some of the birds in a dark color first and work on top with gold when dry. This also helps to give the bird shapes a well-defined outside edge.

Ducks & chickens lattice variations

This project seems to suit muted earth tones best, but you could try any combination of colors. The feathers would look especially good in bright hues as an all-over wall design, floating and drifting on the surface. You could stencil the ducks and chickens in regimental rows or place them randomly as if waddling and pecking round the farmyard.

Quills border (stencil D)

Birds Frieze
(stencils A and C)

Lattice tile (stencil F)

Feathers motif (stencil D)

Birds and lattice edging (stencils A, C and E)

Lattice edging (stencil E)

Lattice frieze (stencil E)

Floating feathers (stencil B)

Above: Chicken roundelay (stencils A and F)

Lattice corner (stencil F)

Patchwork tablecloth

Red and white checks seem to conjure up the instant warmth of a farmhouse.

With just a few basic shapes, combined totally at random, it is easy to create a

pattern that looks a great deal more complicated than it really is. This project

requires patience in planning, but the end result is incredibly satisfying —

a tablecloth that is crying out for a steaming pot of tea and copious quantities

of home-made cookies and jam to be set upon it.

PAINT COLOR GUIDE

Bright red

Cream

White

PAINTING THE TROMPE L'OEIL CLOTH

1 Map out freehand with a faint pencil line where you want the tablecloth to be. If you are working on bare wood, prime it. Paint the base color of the cloth in a cream-colored latex.

2 When dry load up a paintbrush with the same cream color and paint a ridge on the edge of the cloth. Do this by slightly twisting the brush outwards, away from the cloth towards the wood. Paint in a white line to finish the edge.

3 Stencil the solid red square shapes first (stencil G).

4 Fill in the empty squares at random. Stand back every so often to check that the different elements are evenly distributed.

5 Stencil a line of stitches (stencil B) along the outside edge. Finally, varnish the cloth.

PROJECT PATTERN

The pattern in the photograph on the previos page is built up of alternating red squares and motifs of your choice in between.

G   A   G

H   F

G   C   G

PAINTING THE EDGE OF THE CLOTH

To make the cloth look more three-dimensional, paint a ridge on the outside edge and finish it off with a thin white line. This will give the illusion that the cloth is sitting on top of the table rather than painted on.

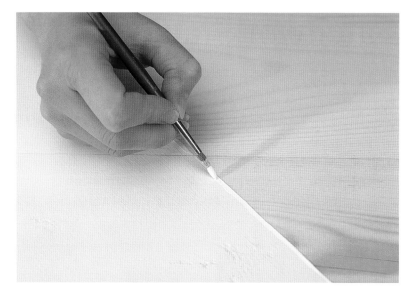

MARKING OUT THE SQUARES

Find the centre of the cloth and draw inside stencil G in pencil to mark out the first square. Draw lines across the square from corner to corner and extend them to the edge of the cloth. Mark 5¼" (13 cm) intervals along these lines. Following the direction of the first square, link the lines together to create a grid, enabling you to position the stencil card easily.

PLACING THE MOTIFS

Stencil the non-symmetrical shapes in all directions so that they can be viewed from all angles. For example, position a heart facing up in one square, down in the next, or left and right. Finally, rub out any remaining lines and put on a couple of layers of varnish. An oil-based varnish makes the surface slightly heat resistant and gives a yellow tinge, which unifies the whole surface.

Patchwork tablecloth variations

By painting the patchwork design in blue and yellow ochre you can create a softer look, perhaps lifted with just a little red for warmth. An unusual variation would be to paint a wallhanging using the double stitch (stencil D) as fringing. The motifs can be used to give impact in small areas and in more muted shades they could be used to create a Shaker-style design.

Square and heart motif (stencils A and G)

Star tiles (stencil H)

Below: Stitched heart border (stencils A and D)

Hearts stripes
(stencils A
and C)

Square and windmill blocks (stencils F and G)

Star and stitch border (stencils B, G and H)

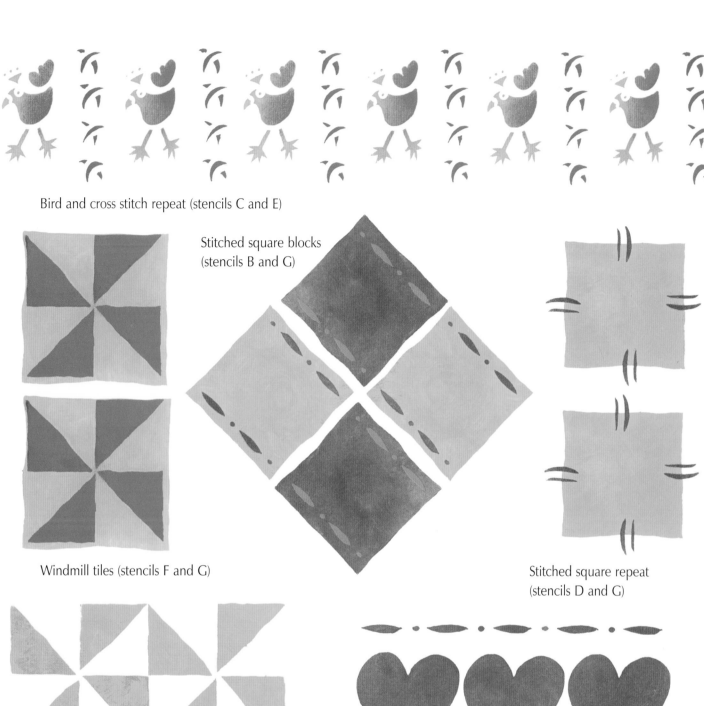

Bird and cross stitch repeat (stencils C and E)

Stitched square blocks
(stencils B and G)

Windmill tiles (stencils F and G)

Stitched square repeat
(stencils D and G)

Windmill blocks (stencil F)

Reflected hearts border (stencils A and B)

Herbs & ribbon

The calm, muted colors of sage green, clear blue and purple are ideal for creating a gentle rustic theme. Freshly gathered herbs tied together in bunches with a colorful purple ribbon and hanging from the kitchen beams to dry, conjure up the essence of country life. Sage, rosemary and thyme are all plants stored for use during the winter months for culinary purposes or herbal remedies, lotions and potions. Here they decorate the shelves and a wooden platter.

PAINT COLOR GUIDE

Cream
Sage green
Cornflower blue
Purple

DECORATING THE PLATTER

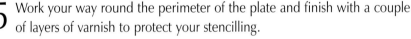

1 Paint the wooden plate with primer and then with a coat of cream latex.

2 Mix a small amount of sage green latex paint with flat glaze and apply a wash to the plate using big sweeping movements.

3 Start the stencilling with the ribbon (stencil A) and build up the herbs from the bottom. Fill any gaps with sections of the stencils.

4 Use different gradations of color to give variation and depth to the design.

5 Work your way round the perimeter of the plate and finish with a couple of layers of varnish to protect your stencilling.

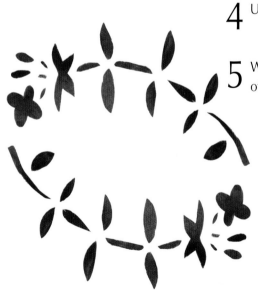

The border on the plate in the photograph on the previous page is a simple repeat of this pattern; stencils are superimposed in a random manner to create the bunch of herbs in the centre.

E

F

MASKING OFF PARTS OF STENCILS

In this project the design is built up as you go along, sometimes using the whole shape of the stencil and sometimes masking off sections to fill in the gaps. Do not worry if shapes overlap — it adds to the end result and makes the herb bunch look more generous.

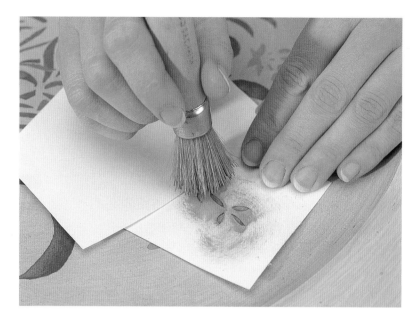

MEASURING FOR THE BORDER

To have a set repeat round the outside of the plate you will need to measure the design you want to use, then measure the space you want it to fit into. Simply divide the design length into the plate circumference and mark it onto the plate faintly in pencil as a guide. Use a tape measure for measuring.

GRADUATING COLOR FOR DEPTH

By graduating the paint color from light to dark within the stencil and repeating this in each subsequent shape you can achieve an undulating effect. This will give your design more visual movement.

Herbs & ribbon variations

Sage green is a color that seems instantly to suggest a country kitchen, but a much brighter blue-green is used here to good effect. The shape of the thyme sprigs allows them to be trailed wherever you wish and although the rosemary and sage are slightly more rigid in pattern they can also be placed in a multitude of designs. Bunches of herbs would look great stencilled as if hanging just below the ceiling.

Reflected stalk frieze (stencil C)

Twisted thyme border (stencil E)

Sage leaf edging (stencil D)

Entwined ribbons border (stencil A)

Above: Ribbon edging (stencil A)

Sage leaf border (stencil D)

Reflected stalk edging (stencil C)

Sage leaf pattern (stencil D)

Rosemary border (stencil B)

Looped ribbon
bow (stencil A)

Thyme swag (stencil F)

Thyme circle (stencil F)

Random ribbons (stencil A)

NATURE'S
HARVEST

These designs celebrate the abundance of nature. The many different forms of fruits and flowers give designers a wonderful range of shapes, textures and colors to experiment with. Try a Mediterranean feel with a Tuscan olive pattern, or a touch of France with Provençal figs and clematis. Whatever the room, you're sure to find a pattern for it among these glorious shapes.

Spring lilies & crab apples

Delicate white lilies are traditionally associated with modesty and purity, but they make an effective contrast with the familiar culinary properties of acid green crab apples. To create an instant impression of peace and harmony you could use any of these stencils in different combinations. There are no hard and fast rules, so move the stencils as your space dictates. Transform a plain kitchen wall, as here, or perhaps trail the shapes over your garden furniture and containers.

PAINT COLOR GUIDE

White

Lime green

Dark green

PAINTING THE BORDER

1 First paint your wall with apple-green latex paint.

2 Carefully mark out the border using a carpenter's level and mask off the stencilling area with low-tack tape or string pinned at intervals.

3 Gently spray the backs of the stencils with spray adhesive, leave for a few minutes so the glue is not too sticky, then start to put them in position.

4 Position your stencils randomly, trying not to repeat the same motif next to itself. Place them at varying angles — even sideways or upside down. Reposition them until you are happy with the pattern.

A

B

C

D

E

PAINTING LIGHT ON DARK

It is usual to start with a light background and paint darker colored stencils. Here the combination of light on dark and dark on light adds to the depth of the design. To work with white use a clean sponge and dry stencil.

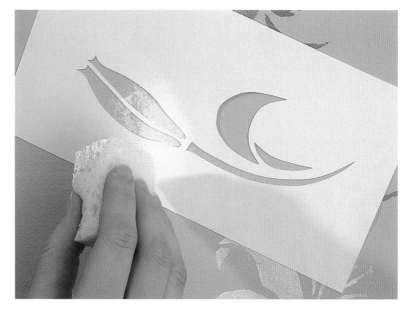

FADING FOR AN AGED LOOK

A fresco effect can be achieved by fading colors into the background. In this way the end result will not look so contrived and the stencilled image will look as if it has been on the wall for years.

BALANCING THE DESIGN

Placing the stencils randomly may seem an easy option, but it requires careful planning. Take the time to stand back and see that the weight of the design is level. Fiddle with the different elements in the empty spaces until one fits.

Spring lillies & crab apples variations

Instead of the cool effect of the lime-green and white combination used on the kitchen wall, try a variation. How about burgundy lilies with more muted green crab apples, for example? Use the lilies on their own or leave the crab apples cooking in rows. For a more sophisticated setting try the designs in a dining room.

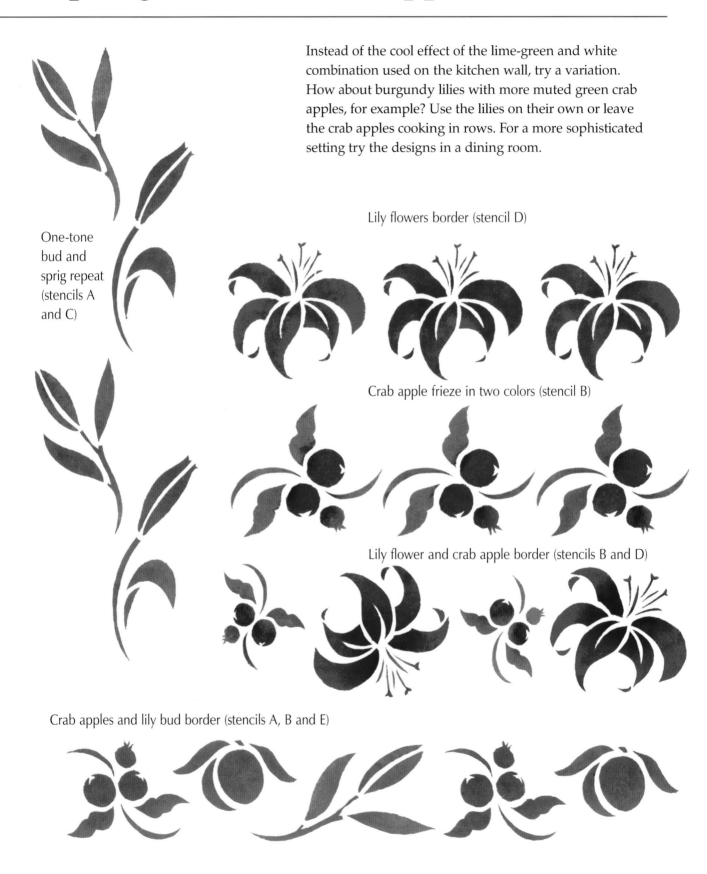

One-tone bud and sprig repeat (stencils A and C)

Lily flowers border (stencil D)

Crab apple frieze in two colors (stencil B)

Lily flower and crab apple border (stencils B and D)

Crab apples and lily bud border (stencils A, B and E)

Simple linking sprigs (stencil C)

Large crab apple border (stencil E)

Twisting crab apple frieze (stencil B)

Bold flower pattern (stencil D)

Lily Art Deco design (stencil C)

Lily flower and bud repeat (stencils A and D)

Simple linking buds (stencil A)

Provençal figs & clematis

The balmy atmosphere of the South of France is conjured up by this attractive

combination of luscious figs and the stately appearance of large clematis blooms.

Earthy colors of dark terra cotta, purple, olive and cream epitomize fall in Provence.

Create a warm and rustic look on anything from blanket boxes to archways,

study walls to kitchen cabinets. The trailing nature of the clematis plant, with its

star-shaped flowers and entwining tendrils, particularly lends itself to floors.

PAINT COLOR GUIDE

Deep purple

Terra cotta

Olive green

Golden cream

Dark brown

PAINTING THE FLOOR PATTERN

1 First whitewash the floorboards with a 50:50 mix of water and white latex paint. Build up in layers until you have the desired effect.

2 Position the stencil cards on the floor. Try to keep the pattern looking like it is growing so that it engulfs the surface.

3 Alternate the leaves with tendrils, flowers and figs totally at random. If you come across a good combination, repeat it, but at a good distance from the first so that you achieve a natural-looking effect. Floors should be finished off with a couple of coats of varnish.

MOTTLED LEAVES

To achieve a mottled look within each element, dab the stencil with one color, let it dry for a moment, then sponge a different color on top. This gives a wonderful uneven effect.

SHADING THE FIGS

Create graduated shading by blending into the first color while it is still wet. Start with the darker color, but do not put it quite as far as you ultimately want it to go. Then work back towards this with the lighter color.

TACKLING CORNERS

Work around corners in as flowing a manner as possible. Sometimes it helps to put an element such as a tendril in the corner to give definition. Stand back as you progress to check you are maintaining the feeling of movement.

Provençal figs and clematis variations

As a contrast to the ripening purple figs used as a floor decoration, try a more subdued color scheme. For a lighter effect combine olive green figs with creamy white clematis blooms. Perhaps you could paint the design growing along the floor over the skirting board and up the wall. The motifs could also be used as all-over hand-painted "wallpaper" designs.

Figs and tendrils border (stencils C and F)

Leaf block border (stencil B)

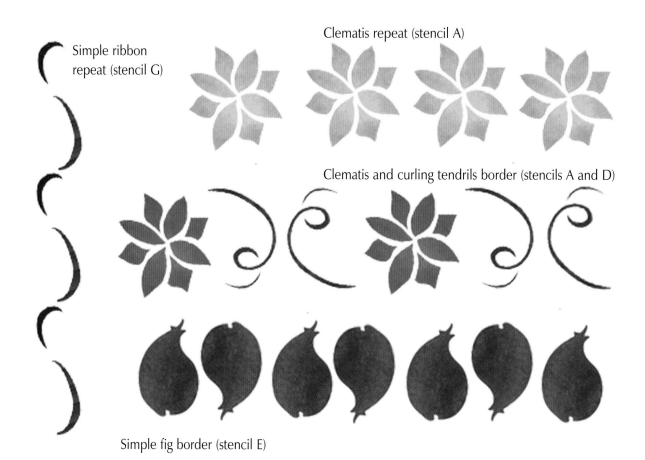

Simple ribbon repeat (stencil G)

Clematis repeat (stencil A)

Clematis and curling tendrils border (stencils A and D)

Simple fig border (stencil E)

Leaf, ribbon and fig pattern (stencils B, C and G)

Tendril edging
(stencil F)

Figs and curling tendrils (stencils C, D and E)

Tendril repeat (stencil F)

Fig border (stencil C)

Tumbling leaves
(stencil B)

Clematis flower border (stencils A and G)

Tuscan olives

Enjoy long summer evenings over a meal around this patio table. Stencilled with plump Mediterranean olives, it brings the flavour and atmosphere of Tuscany to your own home. The table is painted in traditional Tuscan earth colors that are rich and warm, and provide an authentic-looking background for the border of olives. It has been finished with an antiquing varnish that enhances the colors and gives it an aged look. A final coat of clear varnish protects the surface.

PAINT COLOR GUIDE

Mustard yellow

Terra cotta

Olive green

Yellow-green

Dark green

Brown

Black

PREPARING AND FINISHING THE TABLE

1 Paint the table with two coats of mustard yellow latex paint. Make a glaze using acrylic scumble and terra-cotta paint. Using a soft cloth, pick up some glaze and rub it over the tabletop to give it a textured finish. The base color should now show through the glaze. After stencilling, apply antiquing varnish.

2 Plan the positions of the stencilling by measuring carefully. Design a one-eighth segment around the table to check the fit.

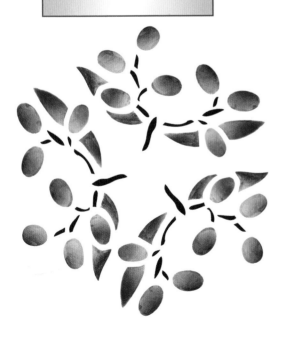

A

POSITIONING THE OLIVE STENCIL

Plan the positions of your stencils around the edge of the table top. Careful measuring at the start will ensure that you are not left with either too much or too little space to complete the circle. First work out how a one-eighth segment will look.

PAINTING THE OLIVES

Use a different brush for each color. Load the tip of the brush, removing excess paint on kitchen paper. Apply the paint by tapping or "pouncing" or, for a smoother look, press lightly on the bristles and use a circular motion.

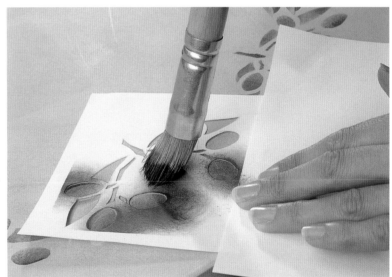

SHADING

Solid blocks of color will appear flat and heavy, so highlight one side of each olive with lighter green paint, making the olives appear round. Use two greens on the leaves to give a more realistic effect.

Tuscan olives variations

Use a single stencil to make a repeating border or combine parts of the designs for a geometric all-over pattern. To make a square tile design, paint the line stencil as a frame using the ends as a link. Position the leaf stencils inside some of the squares. The variations illustrated here show how the use of color can give quite different effects.

Leaf spray (stencil F)

Circle of olives (stencil A)

Flower border (stencil E)

Leaves edging (stencil F)

Flower border (stencil E)

Flower and broken line border (stencils D and E)

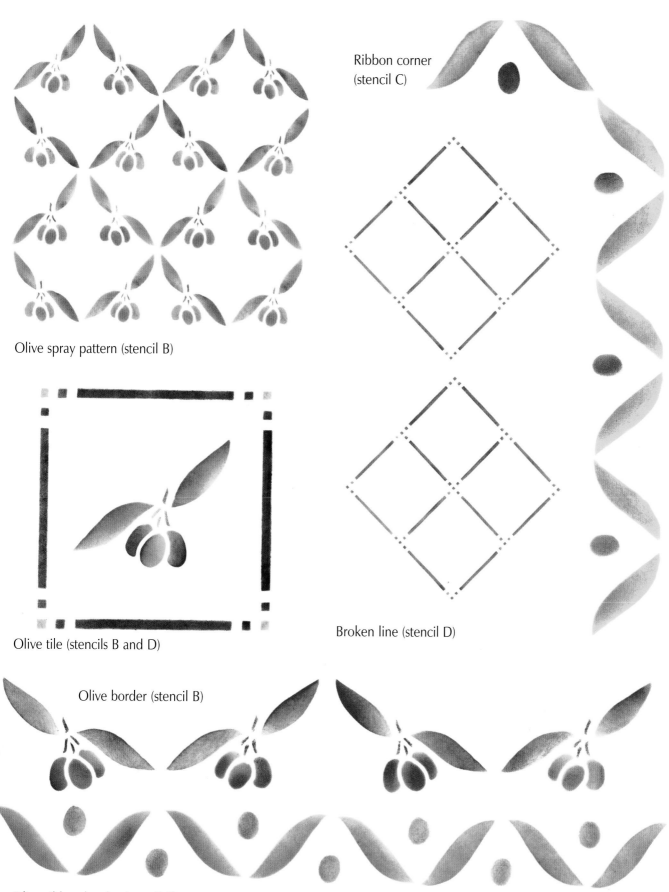

Olive spray pattern (stencil B)

Ribbon corner
(stencil C)

Olive tile (stencils B and D)

Broken line (stencil D)

Olive border (stencil B)

Olive ribbon border (stencil C)

Chinese pomegranates

The familiar Chinese willow pattern inspired this design of pomegranates with flowers and leaves, and its cool blue-and-white color scheme is particularly suitable for a bathroom. The motifs can be used throughout the room — on the walls, the laundry basket, the bath panels and even the windows. They make a dramatic-looking design when positioned closely together to create a border. Individual elements could also be used to simulate hand-blocked wallpaper using a symmetrical pattern.

PAINT COLOR GUIDE
Bright blue

DECORATING THE BATH

1 Paint the side of the bath with a couple of coats of white paint.

2 Position the solid pomegranate (stencil E) first, then put in a leaf and flower, making sure they do not touch. Then position the more delicate fruit (stencil C) at an angle. Follow this with a couple of flowers and a leaf.

3 Trace the pattern to make the repeating process simpler. Slide the stencils under the trace to the right position and remove it to paint. Draw the position of the previous repeat onto the tracing paper to align the repeats correctly.

SQUARING UP

Rather than spending hours putting plumb lines on the bath, use masking tape to stick a mini carpenter's level on the side of the bath. Then you can align and square up your stencil with the level. This makes repositioning much easier.

REVERSING THE COLOR SCHEME

If you are working with a two color scheme, it is fun to paint the combination somewhere in the room the opposite way round. Dramatically contrasting colors work well, but use the technique with similar tones for a more subtle look.

STENCILLING ON WINDOWS

A lovely finish to the scheme can be achieved, especially in bathrooms, if you take the design onto the windows. Mark off the area around the stencil with newspaper and gently spray clear or white spray — this gives a frosted or etched look.

Chinese pomegranates variations

Experiment in your bathroom with a different interpretation of the pomegranate design using aquatints of turquoise and cobalt. Ring the changes with a variation along the same theme. Choosing the right paint for the surface is always tricky. If you want to stencil an uneven surface such as wicker, use a spray paint. Spray evenly using thin coats, to keep the edges of the image well defined.

Twisting pomegranate flowers (stencil B)

Whole pomegranate border (stencil E)

Leaves repeat (stencil F)

Simple flower repeat (stencil A)

Flowing leaves repeat (stencil D)

Floating leaves
(stencils D and F)

Whole pomegranate and flowers repeat (stencils A, B and E)

Pomegranate tile design (stencil C)

Pomegranate tile design (stencil C)

Pomegranate flowers border (stencils A and B)

Published in 2005 by Bay Books,
an imprint of Murdoch Books Pty Limited

www.murdochbooks.com.au

Printed by Sing Cheong Printing Company Ltd. PRINTED IN CHINA.
First printed in 2005. Reprinted 2006.

Dandelions

Sunshine daisies

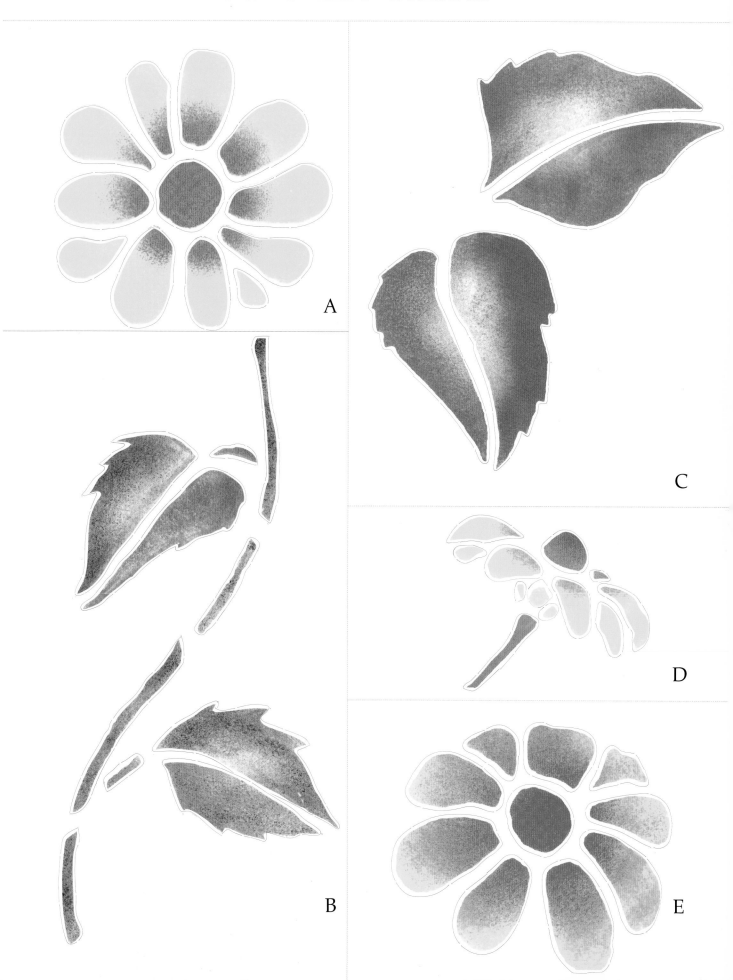

A

C

B

D

E

Poppies

A

B

C

D

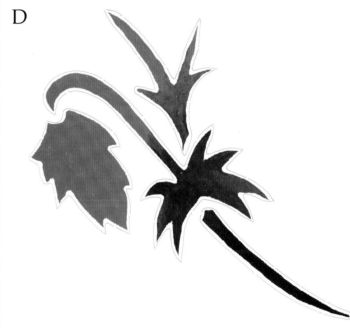

E

F

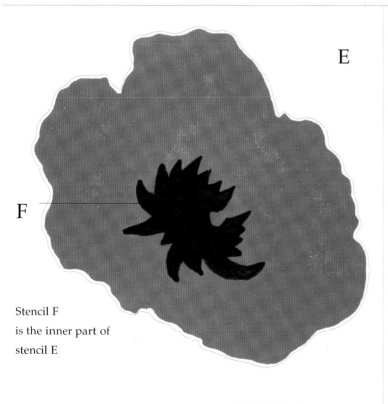

Stencil F
is the inner part of
stencil E

G

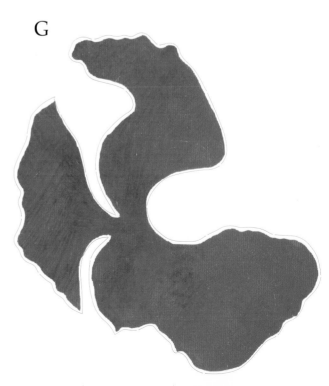

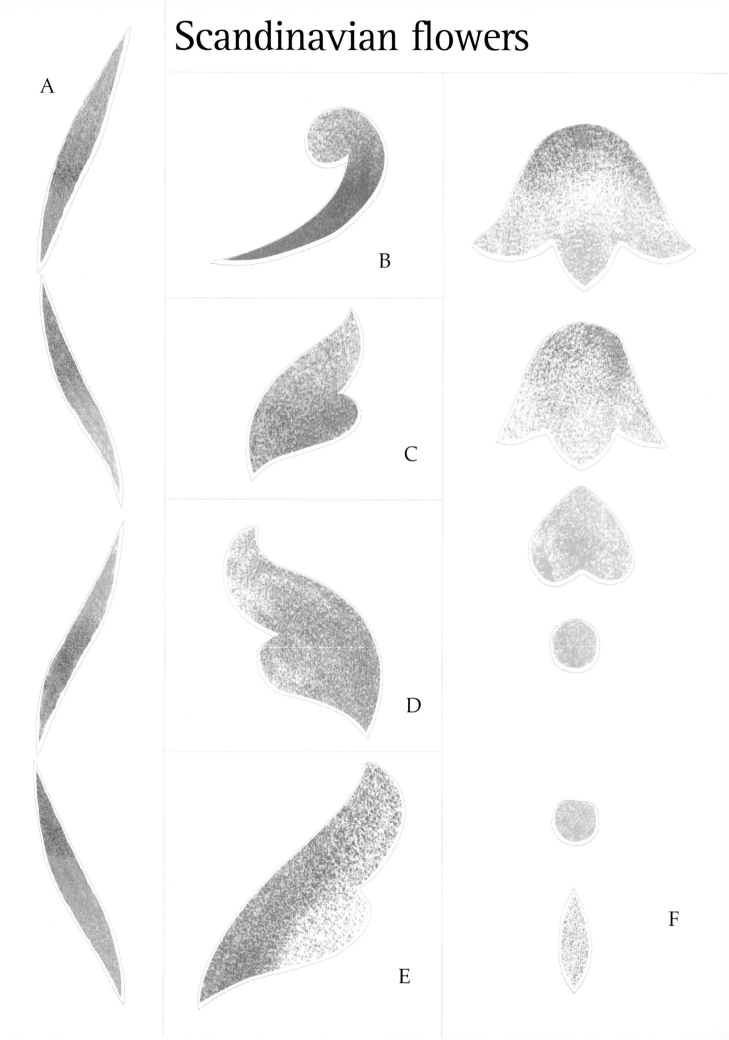

Scandinavian flowers

A

B

C

D

E

F

Fall hedgerow

A

D

B

C

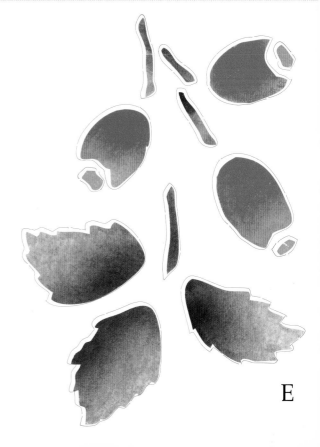

E

Duck & chicken lattice

Patchwork tablecloth

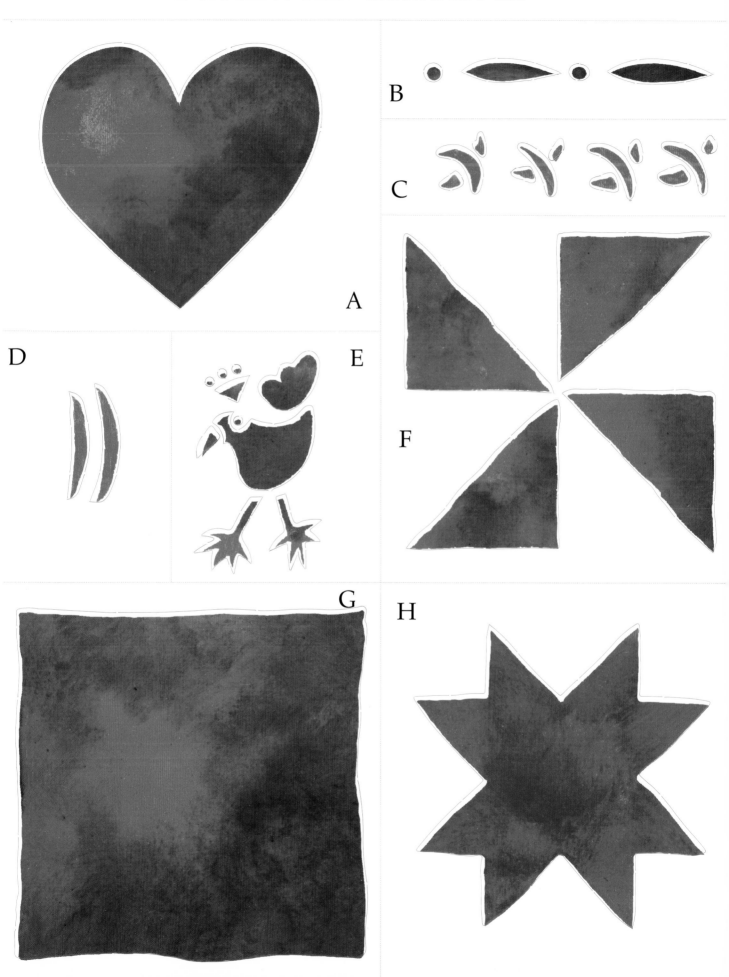

Herbs & ribbon

A

B

C

D

E

F

Spring lilies & crab apples

A

C

(Stencil reversed)

B

D

E

Provençal figs & clematis

Tuscan olives

A

C

B

D

E

F

Chinese pomegranates

A B

C D

E F